NEED OF THE HOUR: LEGISLATIVE REFORMS TO PREVENT MOB LYNCHING

VOLUME 1, ISSUE 4 OF BRILLOPEDIA

SAJIDUR RAHMAN

ISBN 979-888546337-9

Contents

Preface

"Start writing, no matter what. The water does not flow until the faucet is turned on".

-Louis L'Amour

Hundreds of students and professors are contributing their work to Brillopedia, we are here to provide ample information about Law and Contemporary issues. Our aim is to provide a platform for today's generation to express their views and ideas on law and contemporary law.

Publication

This research paper is published in volume 1, issue 4 of Brillopedia

CHAPTER ONE

Abstract

In India, mob lynching is not a new phenomenon. Responsible individuals in India are concerned about the rise in mob lynchings under various pretexts. responsible citizens are concerned about the escalation of mob lynching under various pretexts. Lynching is a premeditated extrajudicial killing by a group. It is most often used to characterize informal public executions by a mob to punish an alleged transgressor or to intimidate a group. It can also be an extreme form of informal group social control, and it is often conducted with the display of a public spectacle for maximum intimidation. In India, there is no codified law against mob lynching, however, provisions of the Indian Penal Code (IPC) and Criminal Procedure Code (CrPC) are applied to deal with instances of mob killing. In this paper, the researcher has attempted to ensure that a legal mechanism is set up in curbing the menace.

Keywords: Mob Lynching, Violence, Legality

CHAPTER TWO

Introduction

When it comes to mob lynching in India, the 21ˢᵗ century is very far from progressive. Mob lynching is becoming more common in India. India's responsible citizens are concerned about the escalation of mob lynching under various pretexts. History is replete with episodes of community violence not only in cities but also in villages, within communities, and across entire regions, with unrestrained and devastating violence in many locations and for reasons known only to the mob.

In India, mob lynching is not a new phenomenon. Many times, the mob erupts into violence in a matter of seconds, without pausing to consider the underlying issue that has stirred the mob's attention. The word lynching originated in the United States in the mid-18ᵗʰ century. Historians believe that the term was first used by planter Charles Lynch to describe extra-judicial authority assumed by private individuals like him. It came to be applied over time to extra-judicial killings by crowds, most commonly of African-Americans in the late 19ᵗʰ century.[1] Although the word lynching is of foreign origin, this does not mean that mob lynchings are alien to India.

A lynch mob may be defined as a form of violence in which a mob, under the pretext of administering justice without trial, executes a presumed offender, often after inflicting torture and corporal mutilation. The term lynch refers to a self-constituted court that imposes a sentence on a person without due process of law. It is a culmination of individuals taking the law into their own hands as a means of achieving justice.[i] Aptly referred to by the Hon'ble Supreme Court as a "horrendous act of mobocracy" mob lynchings have a pattern and a motive.[2] More often than not, innocent people are targeted based on some rumor, misinformation, or suspicion.

[1] James Allen, *Lynchin in America: Confronting the Legacy of Racial Terror,* (Dec. 5,2021. 10:04 AM), https://lynchinginamerica.eji.org/report/

[2]*Sociology of Mob Lynching,* (Dec. 5,2021. 10:14 AM), http://www.azadindia.org/social-issues/view-soc-news.php?id=3

CHAPTER THREE

Mob lynching in India: A threat to mankind

In recent years, there has been a significant increase in mob lynchings in India. In yet another case of mob lynching, Animesh Bhuyan, a 30-year-old leader of the All Assam Students Union (AASU), was lynched to death by an enraged crowd on November 29, 2021, in Jorhat, Assam owing to miscommunication. Two other youths Pranay Dutta (an AASU activist) and Mridusmanta Baruah (former AASU leader and a correspondent of Pratidin Time) were also injured in the incident and were rushed to Jorhat Medical College and Hospital (JMCH) immediately.

In India, there is no codified law against mob lynching, however, provisions of the Indian Penal Code (IPC) are applied to deal with instances of mob killing like murder[i], attempt to murder[1], causing voluntary hurt[2], grievous hurt[3], rioting[4], rioting armed with deadly weapons[5], unlawful assembly[6]. Similarly, according to the Criminal Procedure Code (CrPC), it is allowed to try two or more accused of conducting a crime as the same transaction.[7] It should be noted, that despite the prevalence of sections under the IPC and CrPC to prosecute mob killings, legal experts have suggested the need for separate legislation to tackle mob killings in India. People taking the law into their own hands in a country like India is unacceptable since citizens of the country have been granted several fundamental rights, and such lynching situations violate their right to life, right to a fair trial, and so on.

In the year 2017, The Protection of Lynching Act, 2017 also known as the Manav Suraksha Kanoon Bill[8] (MASUKA) put forth by the National Campaign against Mob Lynching (NCAML), defined, for the first time in Indian legal history, the terms "lynching", "mob" and "victim". It was introduced in the Rajya Sabha as a private member's bill. It reconciles the definition of the term "mob" as mentioned in the IPC and CrPC to require five or more persons as opposed to this Bill, wherein, two or more persons resorting to violence by extrajudicial means would constitute a mob.

In July 2018, the Supreme Court, while pronouncing its judgment in the case of *Tahseen S. Poonawala* v. *Union of India*[9], Hon'ble Chief Justice of India, Dipak Mishra along with the three-judge bench had laid down several preventive, remedial, and punitive measures to deal with lynching and mob violence. States were ordered to establish special fast track courts in each district to deal solely with instances involving mob lynchings. The court had also recommended forming a special task force to collect information on those involved in spreading hate speeches, inflammatory comments, and fake news that might lead to mob lynchings and to appoint a senior police officer as a nodal officer in each district to take preventative measures against mob violence and lynching. The nodal officers are to hold monthly meetings with local intelligence units and the Director-General of Police of the state or Secretary, Home Department, must, in turn, hold regular review meetings with nodal officers to curb such instances of vigilantism by mobs.

In addition, instructions were issued to establish victim compensation systems for the relief and rehabilitation of victims. A year later, in July 2019, the Supreme Court issued notices to the Centre and several states, urging that they submit their progress toward implementing the measures as well as compliance reports. The states lethargic response was exceedingly disappointing. As of now, only three states Manipur, West Bengal, and Rajasthan have enacted laws against mob lynching.

[1] The Indian Penal Code, 1860, s. 300

[2]*Ibid*, s. 323

[3]*Ibid*, s. 147

[4]*Ibid*, s. 148

[5]*Ibid*, s. 149

[6] The Criminal Procedure Code, 1973, s. 223(a)

[7]*Draft law of Manav Suraksha Kanoon' (MASUKA) –National Campaign Against Mob Lynching*, (Dec. 7, 2021. 10:04 AM), https://blog.ipleaders.in/draft-law-manav-suraksha-kanoon-masuka-national-campaign-mob-lynching/#_ftn8.

[8]*Supra* note 4.

[9] Krishnamoorthy v. Sivakumar and others 2015 3 SCC 467, (India).

CHAPTER FOUR

Way Forward

Cases of mob lynching are increasing day by day, be it the killing of 16 years old Jhankar Saikia in Karbi Anglong district's Diphu, Nilotpal Das, Abhijeet Nath, in Karbi Anglong, **Akhlaq lynching case, Palghar lynching case or Dhule lynching case, etc.** The need of the hour is to pass legislation to prohibit mob lynchings and honour killings. When it comes to mob lynchings in India, numerous reforms must be considered. Coupled with the guidelines laid down in Poonawala's case, we are sufficiently equipped to deal with mob lynching. However, what we lack is due enforcement of the existing laws and the accountability of the enforcement agencies. The administration must take efforts to guarantee that justice is delivered more quickly.

The parliament can play an essential role in improving mob lynching legislation. The parliament should act in accordance with the Supreme Courts directions, and accordingly draft a new law to deal with cases involving mob lynching, intending to provide a maximum penalty to lynchers as well as authorities who are directly or indirectly involved in mob lynching instances. Further, the new law must define the term "mob lynching" which is not defined in any of the current statutes.

Moreover, a mechanism should be set up to ensure that justice has been delivered to the victims of mob violence. The government should take appropriate steps to pass law demanded by Civil Society, Manav Suraksha Kanoon (MASUKA) which provides that stringent laws should be made for mob violence, and also laws related to mob lynching must be non-bailable, cognizable, and non-compoundable, and also invite life imprisonment along with a time-bound trial of the culprit. Moreover, compensation to the families of victims and the police action must be considered to ensure the protection of the witnesses.

Mob lynching is a heinous stain on our legal system. It is based on the twisted concept of vigilantism and leads to anarchy. Such excrescence must be strangled with an iron fist. In a civilized society, the most powerful sovereign is the rule of law. The majesty of law cannot be sullied simply because an individual or a group generate the attitude that they have been empowered by the principles set out in law to take its enforcement into their own hands and gradually become a law unto themselves and punish the violator on their assumption and in the manner in which they deem fit[1]. The rule of law has to be upheld for any civilized society to endure.